ON THE SHORTNESS
OF LIFE

LUCIUS ANNAEUS SENECA

Translated by
AUBREY STEWART

To Paulinus[1].

CONTENTS

I

The greater part of mankind, my Paulinus, complains of the unkindness of Nature, because we are born only for a short space of time, and that this allotted period of life runs away so swiftly, nay so hurriedly, that with but few exceptions men's life comes to an end just as they are preparing to enjoy it: nor is it only the common herd and the ignorant vulgar who mourn over this universal misfortune, as they consider it to be: this reflection has wrung complaints even from great men. Hence comes that well-known saying of physicians, that art is long but life is short: hence arose that quarrel, so unbefitting a sage, which Aristotle picked with Nature, because she had indulged animals with such length of days that some of them lived for ten or fifteen centuries, while man, although born for many and such great exploits, had the term of his existence cut so much shorter. We do not have a very short time assigned to us, but we lose a great deal of it: life is long enough to carry out the most important projects: we have an ample portion, if we do but arrange the whole of it aright: but when it all runs to waste through luxury and carelessness, when it is not devoted to any good purpose, then at the last we are forced to feel that it is all over, although we never noticed how it glided away. Thus it is: we do not receive a short life, but we make it a short one, and we are not poor in days, but wasteful of them. When great and kinglike riches fall into the hands of a bad master, they are dispersed straightaway, but even a moderate fortune, when bestowed upon a wise guardian, increases by use: and in like manner our life has great opportunities for one who knows how to dispose of it to the best advantage.

II

Why do we complain of Nature? she has dealt kindly with us. Life is long enough, if you know how to use it. One man is possessed by an avarice which nothing can satisfy, another by a laborious diligence in doing what is totally useless: another is sodden by wine: another is benumbed by sloth: one man is exhausted by an ambition which makes him court the good will of others[1]: another, through his eagerness as a merchant, is led to visit every land and every sea by the hope of gain: some are plagued by the love of soldiering, and are always either endangering other men's lives or in trembling for their own: some wear away their lives in that voluntary slavery, the unrequited service of great men: many are occupied either in laying claim to other men's fortune or in complaining of their own: a great number have no settled purpose, and are tossed from one new scheme to another by a rambling, inconsistent, dissatisfied, fickle habit of mind: some care for no object sufficiently to try to attain it, but lie lazily yawning until their fate comes upon them: so that I cannot doubt the truth of that verse which the greatest of poets has dressed in the guise of an oracular response—

"We live a small part only of our lives."

But all duration is time, not life: vices press upon us and surround us on every side, and do not permit us to regain our feet, or to raise our eyes and gaze upon truth, but when we are down keep us prostrate and chained to low desires. Men who are in this condition are never allowed to come to themselves: if ever by chance they obtain any rest, they roll to and fro like the deep sea, which heaves and tosses after a gale, and they never have any respite from their lusts. Do you suppose that I speak of those whose ills are notorious? Nay, look at those whose prosperity all men run to see: they are choked by their own good things. To how many men do riches prove a heavy burden? how many men's eloquence and continual desire to display their own cleverness has cost them their lives[2]? how many are sallow with constant sensual indulgence? how many have no freedom left them by the tribe of clients that surges around them?

Look through all these, from the lowest to the highest:—this man calls his friends to support him, this one is present in court, this one is the defendant, this one pleads for him, this one is on the jury: but no one lays claim to his own self, everyone wastes his time over someone else. Investigate those men, whose names are in everyone's mouth: you will find that they bear just the same marks: A is devoted to B, and B to C: no one belongs to himself. Moreover some men are full of most irrational anger: they complain of the insolence of their chiefs, because they have not granted them an audience when they wished for it; as if a man had any right to complain of being so haughtily shut out by another, when he never has leisure to give his own conscience a hearing. This chief of yours, whoever he is, though he may look at you in an offensive manner, still will some day look at you, open his ears to your words, and give you a seat by his side: but you never design to look upon yourself, to listen to your own grievances. You ought not, then, to claim these services from another, especially since while you yourself were doing so, you did not wish for an interview with another man, but were not able to obtain one with yourself.[3]

III

Were all the brightest intellects of all time to employ themselves on this one subject, they never could sufficiently express their wonder at this blindness of men's minds: men will not allow anyone to establish himself upon their estates, and upon the most trifling dispute about the measuring of boundaries, they betake themselves to stones and cudgels; yet they allow others to encroach upon their lives, nay, they themselves actually lead others in to take possession of them. You cannot find anyone who wants to distribute his money; yet among how many people does everyone distribute his life? men covetously guard their property from waste, but when it comes to waste of time, they are most prodigal of that of which it would become them to be sparing. Let us take one of the elders, and say to him,

"We perceive that you have arrived at the extreme limits of human life: you are in your hundredth year, or even older. Come now, reckon up your whole life in black and white: tell us how much of your time has been spent upon your creditors, how much on your mistress, how much on your king, how much on your clients, how much in quarrelling with your wife, how much in keeping your slaves in order, how much in running up and down the city on business. Add to this the diseases which we bring upon us with our own hands, and the time which has laid idle without any use having been made of it; you will see that you have not lived as many years as you count. Look back in your memory and see how often you have been consistent in your projects, how many days passed as you intended them to do when you were at your own disposal, how often you did not change colour and your spirit did not quail, how much work you have done in so long a time, how many people have without your knowledge stolen parts of your life from you, how much you have lost, how large a part has been taken up by useless grief, foolish gladness, greedy desire, or polite conversation; how little of yourself is left to you: you will then perceive that you will die prematurely." What, then, is the reason of this? It is that people live as though they would live forever: you never remember your human frailty; you never notice how much of your time has already gone by: you spend it as though you had an abundant and overflowing store of it, though all the while that day which you devote to some man or to some thing is perhaps your last. You fear everything, like mortals as you are, and yet you desire everything as if you were immortals. You will hear many men say, "After my fiftieth year I will give myself up to leisure: my sixtieth shall be my last year of public office": and what guarantee have you that your life will last any longer? who will let all this go on just as you have arranged it? are you not ashamed to reserve only the leavings of your life for yourself, and appoint for the enjoyment of your own right mind only that time which you cannot devote to any business? How late it is to begin life just when we have to be leaving it! What a foolish forgetfulness of our mortality, to put off wholesome counsels until our fiftieth or sixtieth year, and to choose that our lives shall begin at a point which few of us ever reach.

IV

You will find that the most powerful and highly-placed men let fall phrases in which they long for leisure, praise it, and prefer it to all the blessings which they enjoy. Sometimes they would fain descend from their lofty pedestal, if it could be safely done: for fortune collapses by its own weight, without any shock or interference from without. The late Emperor Augustus, upon whom the gods bestowed more blessings than on anyone else, never ceased to pray for rest and exemption from the troubles of empire: he used to enliven his labours with this sweet, though unreal consolation, that he would some day live for himself alone. In a letter which he addressed to the Senate, after promising that his rest shall not be devoid of dignity nor discreditable to his former glories, I find the following words:—"These things, however, it is more honourable to do than to promise: but my eagerness for that time, so earnestly longed for, has led me to derive a certain pleasure from speaking about it, though the reality is still far distant."[1] He thought leisure so important, that though he could not actually enjoy it, yet he did so by anticipation and by thinking about it. He, who saw everything depending upon himself alone, who swayed the fortunes of men and of nations, thought that his happiest day would be that on which he laid aside his greatness. He knew by experience how much labour was involved in that glory that shone through all lands, and how much secret anxiety was concealed within it: he had been forced to assert his rights by war, first with his countrymen, next with his colleagues, and lastly with his own relations, and had shed blood both by sea and by land: after marching his troops under arms through Macedonia, Sicily, Egypt, Syria, Asia Minor, and almost all the countries of the world, when they were weary with slaughtering Romans he had directed them against a foreign foe. While he was pacifying the Alpine regions, and subduing the enemies whom he found in the midst of the Roman empire, while he was extending its boundaries beyond the Rhine, the Euphrates, and the Danube, at Rome itself the swords of Murena, Caepio, Lepidus, Egnatius, and others were being sharpened to slay him. Scarcely had he escaped from their plot, when his already failing age was terrified by his daughter and all the noble youths who were pledged to her cause by adultery with her by way of oath of fidelity. Then there was Paulus and Antonius's mistress, a second time to be feared by Rome: and when he had cut out these ulcers from his very limbs, others grew in their place: the empire, like a body overloaded with blood, was always breaking out somewhere. For this reason he longed for leisure: all his labours were based upon hopes and thoughts of leisure: this was the wish of him who could accomplish the wishes of all other men.

V

While tossed hither and thither by Catiline and Clodius, Pompeius and Crassus, by some open enemies and some doubtful friends, while he struggled with the struggling republic and kept it from going to ruin, when at last he was banished, being neither able to keep silence in prosperity nor to endure adversity with patience, how often must Marcus Cicero have cursed that consulship of his which he never ceased to praise, and which nevertheless deserved it? What piteous expressions he uses in a letter to Atticus when Pompeius the father had been defeated, and his son was recruiting his shattered forces in Spain? "Do you ask," writes he, "what I am doing here? I am living in my Tusculan villa almost as a prisoner." He adds more afterwards, wherein he laments his former life, complains of the present, and despairs of the future.

Cicero called himself "half a prisoner," but, by Hercules, the wise man never would have come under so lowly a title: he never would be half a prisoner, but would always enjoy complete and entire liberty, being free, in his own power, and greater than all others: for what can be greater than the man who is greater than Fortune?

VI

When Livius Drusus, a vigorous and energetic man, brought forward bills for new laws and radical measures of the Gracchus pattern, being the centre of a vast mob of all the peoples of Italy, and seeing no way to solve the question, since he was not allowed to deal with it as he wished, and yet was not free to throw it up after having once taken part in it, complained bitterly of his life, which had been one of unrest from the very cradle, and said, we are told, that "he was the only person who had never had any holidays even when he was a boy." Indeed, while he was still under age and wearing the praetexta, he had the courage to plead the cause of accused persons in court, and to make use of his influence so powerfully that it is well known that in some causes his exertions gained a verdict. Where would such precocious ambition stop? You may be sure that one who showed such boldness as a child would end by becoming a great pest both in public and in private life: it was too late for him to complain that he had had no holidays, when from his boyhood he had been a firebrand and a nuisance in the courts. It is a stock question whether he committed suicide: for he fell by a sudden wound in the groin, and some doubted whether his death was caused by his own hand, though none disputed its having happened most seasonably. It would be superfluous to mention more who, while others thought them the happiest of men, have themselves borne true witness to their own feelings, and have loathed all that they have done for all the years of their lives: yet by these complaints they have effected no alteration either in others or in themselves: for after these words have escaped them their feelings revert to their accustomed frame. By Hercules, that life of you great men, even though it should last for more than a thousand years, is still a very short one: those vices of yours would swallow up any extent of time: no wonder if this our ordinary span, which, though Nature hurries on, can be enlarged by common sense, soon slips away from you: for you do not lay hold of it or hold it back, and try to delay the swiftest of all things, but you let it pass as though it were a useless thing and you could supply its place.

VII

Among these I reckon in the first place those who devote their time to nothing but drinking and debauchery: for no men are busied more shamefully: the others, although the glory which they pursue is but a counterfeit, still deserve some credit for their pursuit of it—though you may tell me of misers, of passionate men, of men who hate and who even wage war without a cause—yet all such men sin like men: but the sin of those who are given up to gluttony and lust is a disgraceful one. Examine all the hours of their lives: consider how much time they spend in calculation, how much in plotting, how much in fear, how much in giving and receiving flattery, how much in entering into recognizances for themselves or for others, how much in banquets, which indeed become a serious business, you will see that they are not allowed any breathing time either by their pleasures or their pains. Finally, all are agreed that nothing, neither eloquence nor literature, can be done properly by one who is occupied with something else; for nothing can take deep root in a mind which is directed to some other subject, and which rejects whatever you try to stuff into it. No man knows less about living than a business man: there is nothing about which it is more difficult to gain knowledge. Other arts have many folk everywhere who profess to teach them: some of them can be so thoroughly learned by mere boys, that they are able to teach them to others: but one's whole life must be spent in learning how to live, and, which may perhaps surprise you more, one's whole life must be spent in learning how to die. Many excellent men have freed themselves from all hindrances, have given up riches, business, and pleasure, and have made it their duty to the very end of their lives to learn how to live: and yet the larger portion of them leave this life confessing that they do not yet know how to live, and still less know how to live as wise men. Believe me, it requires a great man and one who is superior to human frailties not to allow any of his time to be filched from him: and therefore it follows that his life is a very long one, because he devotes every possible part of it to himself: no portion lies idle or uncultivated, or in another man's power; for he finds nothing worthy of being exchanged for his time, which he husbands most grudgingly. He, therefore, had time enough: whereas those who gave up a great part of their lives to the people of necessity had not enough. Yet you need not suppose that the latter were not sometimes conscious of their loss: indeed, you will hear most of those who are troubled with great prosperity every now and then cry out amid their hosts of clients, their pleadings in court, and their other honourable troubles, "I am not allowed to live my own life." Why is he not allowed? because all those who call upon you to defend them, take you away from yourself. How many of your days have been spent by that defendant? by that candidate for office? by that old woman who is weary with burying her heirs? by that man who pretends to be ill, in order to excite the greed of those who hope to inherit his property? by that powerful friend of yours, who uses you to swell his train, not to be his friend? Balance your account, and run over all the days of your life; you will see that only a very few days, and only those which were useless for any other purpose, have been left to you. He who has obtained the fasces[1] for which he longed, is eager to get rid of them, and is constantly saying, "When will this year be over?" Another exhibits public games, and once would have given a great deal for the chance of doing so, but now "when," says he, "shall I escape from this?" Another is an advocate who is fought for in all the courts, and who draws immense audiences, who crowd all the forum to a far greater distance than they can hear him; "When," says he, "will vacation-time come?" Every man hurries through his life, and suffers from a yearning for the future, and a weariness of the present: but he who disposes of all his time for his own purposes, who arranges all his days as though he were arranging the plan of his life, neither wishes for nor fears the morrow: for what new pleasure can any hour now bestow upon him? he knows it all, and has indulged in it all even to satiety. Fortune may deal with the rest as she will, his life is already safe from her: such a man may gain something, but cannot lose anything: and, indeed, he can only gain anything in the same way as one who is already glutted and filled can get some extra food which he takes although he does not want it. You have no grounds, therefore, for supposing that anyone has lived long, because he has wrinkles or grey hairs: such a man has not lived long, but has only been long alive. Why! would you think that a man had voyaged much if a fierce gale had caught him as soon as he left his port, and he had been driven round and round the same place continually by a succession of winds blowing from opposite quarters? such a man has not travelled much, he has only been much tossed about.

VIII

I am filled with wonder when I see some men asking others for their time, and those who are asked for it most willing to give it: both parties consider the object for which the time is given, but neither of them thinks of the time itself, as though in asking for this one asked for nothing, and in giving it one gave nothing: we play with what is the most precious of all things: yet it escapes men's notice, because it is an incorporeal thing, and because it does not come before our eyes; and therefore it is held very cheap, nay, hardly any value whatever is put upon it. Men set the greatest store upon presents or pensions, and hire out their work, their services, or their care in order to gain them: no one values time: they give it much more freely, as though it cost nothing. Yet you will see these same people clasping the knees of their physician as suppliants when they are sick and in present peril of death, and if threatened with a capital charge willing to give all that they possess in order that they may live: so inconsistent are they. Indeed, if the number of every man's future years could be laid before him, as we can lay that of his past years, how anxious those who found that they had but few years remaining would be to make the most of them? Yet it is easy to arrange the distribution of a quantity, however small, if we know how much there is: what you ought to husband most carefully is that which may run short you know not when. Yet you have no reason to suppose that they do not know how dear a thing time is: they are wont to say to those whom they especially love that they are ready to give them a part of their own years. They do give them, and know not that they are giving them; but they give them in such a manner that they themselves lose them without the others gaining them. They do not, however, know whence they obtain their supply, and therefore they are able to endure the waste of what is not seen: yet no one will give you back your years, no one will restore them to you again: your life will run its course when once it has begun, and will neither begin again or efface what it has done. It will make no disturbance, it will give you no warning of how fast it flies: it will move silently on: it will not prolong itself at the command of a king, or at the wish of a nation: as it started on its first day, so it will run: it will never turn aside, never delay. What follows, then? Why! you are busy, but life is hurrying on: death will be here some time or other, and you must attend to him, whether you will or no.

IX

Can anything be mentioned which is more insane than the ideas of leisure of those people who boast of their worldly wisdom? They live laboriously, in order that they may live better; they fit themselves out for life at the expense of life itself, and cast their thoughts a long way forwards: yet postponement is the greatest waste of life: it wrings day after day from us, and takes away the present by promising something hereafter: there is no such obstacle to true living as waiting, which loses today while it is depending on the morrow. You dispose of that which is in the hand of Fortune, and you let go that which is in your own. Whither are you looking, whither are you stretching forward? everything future is uncertain: live now straightaway. See how the greatest of bards cries to you and sings in wholesome verse as though inspired with celestial fire:—

"The best of wretched mortals' days is that
Which is the first to fly."

Why do you hesitate, says he, why do you stand back? unless you seize it it will have fled: and even if you do seize it, it will still fly. Our swiftness in making use of our time ought therefore to vie with the swiftness of time itself, and we ought to drink of it as we should of a fast-running torrent which will not be always running. The poet, too, admirably satirizes our boundless thoughts, when he says, not "the first age," but "the first day." Why are you careless and slow while time is flying so fast, and why do you spread out before yourself a vision of long months and years, as many as your greediness requires? he talks with you about one day, and that a fast-fleeting one. There can, then, be no doubt that the best days are those which fly first for wretched, that is, for busy mortals, whose minds are still in their childhood when old age comes upon them, and they reach it unprepared and without arms to combat it. They have never looked forward: they have all of a sudden stumbled upon old age: they never noticed that it was stealing upon them day by day. As conversation, or reading, or deep thought deceives travellers, and they find themselves at their journey's end before they knew that it was drawing near, so in this fast and never-ceasing journey of life, which we make at the same pace whether we are asleep or awake, busy people never notice that they are moving till they are at the end of it.

X

If I chose to divide this proposition into separate steps, supported by evidence, many things occur to me by which I could prove that the lives of busy men are the shortest of all. Fabianus, who was none of your lecture-room philosophers, but one of the true antique pattern, used to say, "We ought to fight against the passions by main force, not by skirmishing, and upset their line of battle by a home charge, not by inflicting trifling wounds: I do not approve of dallying with sophisms; they must be crushed, not merely scratched." Yet, in order that sinners may be confronted with their errors, they must be taught, and not merely mourned for. Life is divided into three parts: that which has been, that which is, and that which is to come: of these three stages, that which we are passing through is brief, that which we are about to pass is uncertain, and that which we have passed is certain: this it is over which Fortune has lost her rights, and which can fall into no other man's power: and this is what busy men lose: for they have no leisure to look back upon the past, and even if they had, they take no pleasure in remembering what they regret: they are, therefore, unwilling to turn their minds to the contemplation of ill-spent time, and they shrink from reviewing a course of action whose faults become glaringly apparent when handled a second time, although they were snatched at when we were under the spell of immediate gratification. No one, unless all his acts have been submitted to the infallible censorship of his own conscience, willingly turns his thoughts back upon the past. He who has ambitiously desired, haughtily scorned, passionately vanquished, treacherously deceived, greedily snatched, or prodigally wasted much, must needs fear his own memory; yet this is a holy and consecrated part of our time, beyond the reach of all human accidents, removed from the dominion of Fortune, and which cannot be disquieted by want, fear, or attacks of sickness: this can neither be troubled nor taken away from one: we possess it forever undisturbed. Our present consists only of single days, and those, too, taken one hour at a time: but all the days of past times appear before us when bidden, and allow themselves to be examined and lingered over, albeit busy men cannot find time for so doing. It is the privilege of a tranquil and peaceful mind to review all the parts of its life: but the minds of busy men are like animals under the yoke, and cannot bend aside or look back. Consequently, their life passes away into vacancy, and as you do no good however much you may pour into a vessel which cannot keep or hold what you put there, so also it matters not how much time you give men if it can find no place to settle in, but leaks away through the chinks and holes of their minds. Present time is very short, so much so that to some it seems to be no time at all; for it is always in motion, and runs swiftly away: it ceases to exist before it comes, and can no more brook delay than can the universe or the host of heaven, whose unresting movement never lets them pause on their way. Busy men, therefore, possess present time alone, that being so short that they cannot grasp it, and when they are occupied with many things they lose even this.

XI

In a word, do you want to know for how short a time they live? see how they desire to live long: broken-down old men beg in their prayers for the addition of a few more years: they pretend to be younger than they are: they delude themselves with their own lies, and are as willing to cheat themselves as if they could cheat Fate at the same time: when at last some weakness reminds them that they are mortal, they die as it were in terror: they may rather be said to be dragged out of this life than to depart from it. They loudly exclaim that they have been fools and have not lived their lives, and declare that if they only survive this sickness they will spend the rest of their lives at leisure: at such times they reflect how uselessly they have laboured to provide themselves with what they have never enjoyed, and how all their toil has gone for nothing: but those whose life is spent without any engrossing business may well find it ample: no part of it is made over to others, or scattered here and there; no part is entrusted to fortune, is lost by neglect, is spent in ostentatious giving, or is useless: all of it is, so to speak, invested at good interest. A very small amount of it, therefore, is abundantly sufficient, and so, when his last day arrives, the wise man will not hang back, but will walk with a steady step to meet death.

XII

Perhaps you will ask me whom I mean by "busy men"? you need not think that I allude only to those who are hunted out of the courts of justice with dogs at the close of the proceedings, those whom you see either honourably jostled by a crowd of their own clients or contemptuously hustled in visits of ceremony by strangers, who call them away from home to hang about their patron's doors, or who make use of the praetor's sales by auction to acquire infamous gains which some day will prove their own ruin. Some men's leisure is busy: in their country house or on their couch, in complete solitude, even though they have retired from all men's society, they still continue to worry themselves: we ought not to say that such men's life is one of leisure, but their very business is sloth. Would you call a man idle who expends anxious finicking care in the arrangement of his Corinthian bronzes, valuable only through the mania of a few connoisseurs? and who passes the greater part of his days among plates of rusty metal? who sits in the palaestra (shame, that our very vices should be foreign) watching boys wrestling? who distributes his gangs of fettered slaves into pairs according to their age and colour? who keeps athletes of the latest fashion? Why do you call those men idle, who pass many hours at the barber's while the growth of the past night is being plucked out by the roots, holding councils over each several hair, while the scattered locks are arranged in order and those which fall back are forced forward on to the forehead? How angry they become if the shaver is a little careless, as though he were shearing a man! what a white heat they work themselves into if some of their mane is cut away, if some part of it is ill-arranged, if all their ringlets do not lie in regular order! who of them would not rather that the state were overthrown than that his hair should be ruffled? who does not care more for the appearance of his head than for his health? who would not prefer ornament to honour? Do you call these men idle, who make a business of the comb and looking-glass? what of those who devote their lives to composing, hearing, and learning songs who twist their voices, intended by Nature to sound best and simplest when used straightforwardly, through all the turns of futile melodies; whose fingers are always beating time to some music on which they are inwardly meditating; who, when invited to serious and even sad business may be heard humming an air to themselves?—such people are not at leisure, but are busy about trifles. As for their banquets, by Hercules, I cannot reckon them among their unoccupied times when I see with what anxious care they set out their plate, how laboriously they arrange the girdles of their waiters' tunics, how breathlessly they watch to see how the cook dishes up the wild boar, with what speed, when the signal is given, the slave-boys run to perform their duties, how skilfully birds are carved into pieces of the right size, how painstakingly wretched youths wipe up the spittings of drunken men. By these means men seek credit for taste and grandeur, and their vices follow them so far into their privacy that they can neither eat nor drink without a view to effect. Nor should I count those men idle who have themselves carried hither and thither in sedans and litters, and who look forward to their regular hour for taking this exercise as though they were not allowed to omit it: men who are reminded by someone else when to bathe, when to swim, when to dine: they actually reach such a pitch of languid effeminacy as not to be able to find out for themselves whether they are hungry. I have heard one of these luxurious folk—if indeed, we ought to give the name of luxury to unlearning the life and habits of a man—when he was carried in men's arms out of the bath and placed in his chair, say inquiringly, "Am I seated?" Do you suppose that such a man as this, who did not know when he was seated, could know whether he was alive, whether he could see, whether he was at leisure? I can hardly say whether I pity him more if he really did not know or if he pretended not to know this. Such people do really become unconscious of much, but they behave as though they were unconscious of much more: they delight in some failings because they consider them to be proofs of happiness: it seems the part of an utterly low and contemptible man to know what he is doing. After this, do you suppose that playwrights draw largely upon their imaginations in their burlesques upon luxury: by Hercules, they omit more than they invent; in this age, inventive in this alone, such a number of incredible vices have been produced, that already you are able to reproach the playwrights with omitting to notice them. To think that there should be anyone who had so far lost his senses through luxury as to take someone else's opinion as to whether he was sitting or not? This man certainly is not at leisure: you must bestow a different title on him: he is sick, or rather dead: he only is at leisure who feels that he is at leisure: but this creature is only half alive, if he wants someone to tell him what position his body is in. How can such a man be able to dispose of any time?

XIII

It would take long to describe the various individuals
who have wasted their lives over playing at draughts,
playing at ball, or toasting their bodies in the sun: men
are not at leisure if their pleasures partake of the character of business, for no one will doubt that those
persons are laborious triflers who devote themselves to
the study of futile literary questions, of whom there is
already a great number in Rome also. It used to be a
peculiarly Greek disease of the mind to investigate how
many rowers Ulysses had, whether the Iliad or the
Odyssey was written first, and furthermore, whether
they were written by the same author, with other
matters of the same stamp, which neither please your
inner consciousness if you keep them to yourself, nor
make you seem more learned, but only more trouble-

some, if you publish them abroad. See, already this vain
longing to learn what is useless has taken hold of the
Romans: the other day I heard somebody telling who
was the first Roman general who did this or that: Duil-
lius was the first who won a sea-fight, Curius Dentatus
was the first who drove elephants in his triumph: moreover, these stories, though they add nothing to real glory,
do nevertheless deal with the great deeds of our countrymen: such knowledge is not profitable, yet it claims
our attention as a fascinating kind of folly. I will even
pardon those who want to know who first persuaded the
Romans to go on board ship. It was Claudius, who for
this reason was surnamed Caudex, because any piece of
carpentry formed of many planks was called caudex by
the ancient Romans, for which reason public records are
called codices, and by old custom the ships which ply on
the Tiber with provisions are called codicariae. Let us
also allow that it is to the point to tell how Valerius
Corvinus was the first to conquer Messana, and first of
the family of the Valerii transferred the name of the
captured city to his own, and was called Messana, and
how the people gradually corrupted the pronunciation
and called him Messalla: or would you let anyone find
interest in Lucius Sulla having been the first to let lions
loose in the circus, they having been previously exhib-
ited in chains, and hurlers of darts having been sent by
King Bocchus to kill them? This may be permitted to

their curiosity: but can it serve any useful purpose to know that Pompeius was the first to exhibit eighteen elephants in the circus, who were matched in a mimic battle with some convicts? The leading man in the State, and one who, according to tradition, was noted among the ancient leaders of the State for his transcendent goodness of heart, thought it a notable kind of show to kill men in a manner hitherto unheard of. Do they fight to the death? that is not cruel enough: are they torn to pieces? that is not cruel enough: let them be crushed flat by animals of enormous bulk. It would be much better that such a thing should be forgotten, for fear that hereafter some potentate might hear of it and envy its refined barbarity. O, how doth excessive prosperity blind our intellects! at the moment at which he was casting so many troops of wretches to be trampled on by outlandish beasts, when he was proclaiming war between such different creatures, when he was shedding so much blood before the eyes of the Roman people, whose blood he himself was soon to shed even more freely, he thought himself the master of the whole world; yet he afterwards, deceived by the treachery of the Alexandrians, had to offer himself to the dagger of the vilest of slaves, and then at last discovered what an empty boast was his surname of "The Great." But to return to the point from which I have digressed, I will prove that even on this very subject some people expend useless pains.

The same author tells us that Metellus, when he triumphed after having conquered the Carthaginians in Sicily, was the only Roman who ever had a hundred and twenty captured elephants led before his car: and that Sulla was the last Roman who extended the pomoerium[1] which it was not the custom of the ancients to extend on account of the conquest of provincial, but only of Italian territory. Is it more useful to know this, than to know that the Mount Aventine, according to him, is outside of the pomoerium, for one of two reasons, either because it was thither that the plebeians seceded, or because when Remus took his auspices on that place the birds which he saw were not propitious: and other stories without number of the like sort, which are either actual falsehoods or much the same as falsehoods? for even if you allow that these authors speak in all good faith, if they pledge themselves for the truth of what they write, still, whose mistakes will be made fewer by such stories? whose passions will be restrained? whom will they make more brave, more just, or more gentlemanly? My friend Fabianus used to say that he was not sure that it was not better not to apply oneself to any studies at all than to become interested in these.

XIV

The only persons who are really at leisure are those who devote themselves to philosophy: and they alone really live: for they do not merely enjoy their own lifetime, but they annex every century to their own: all the years which have passed before them belong to them. Unless we are the most ungrateful creatures in the world, we shall regard these noblest of men, the founders of divine schools of thought, as having been born for us, and having prepared life for us: we are led by the labour of others to behold most beautiful things which have been brought out of darkness into light: we are not shut out from any period, we can make our way into every subject, and, if only we can summon up sufficient strength of mind to overstep the narrow limit of human weakness, we have a vast extent of time wherein to disport ourselves: we may argue with Socrates, doubt with Carneades, repose with Epicurus, overcome human nature with the Stoics, exceed it with the Cynics. Since Nature allows us to commune with every age, why do we not abstract ourselves from our own petty fleeting span of time, and give ourselves up with our whole mind to what is vast, what is eternal, what we share with better men than ourselves? Those who gad about in a round of calls, who worry themselves and others, after they have indulged their madness to the full, and crossed every patron's threshold daily, leaving no open door unentered, after they have hawked about their interested greetings in houses of the most various character—after all, how few people are they able to see out of so vast a city, divided among so many different ruling passions: how many will be moved by sloth, self-indulgence, or rudeness to deny them admittance: how many, after they have long plagued them, will run past them with feigned hurry? how many will avoid coming out through their entrance-hall with its crowds of clients, and will escape by some concealed backdoor? as though it were not ruder to deceive their visitor than to deny him admittance!—how many, half asleep and stupid with yesterday's debauch, can hardly be brought to return the greeting of the wretched man who has broken his own rest in order to wait on that of another, even after his name has been whispered to them for the thousandth time, save by a most offensive yawn of his half-opened lips. We may truly say that those men are pursuing the true path of duty, who wish every day to consort on the most familiar terms with Zeno, Pythagoras, Democritus, and the rest of those high priests of virtue, with Aristotle and with Theophrastus. None of these men will be "engaged," none of these will fail to send you away after visiting him in a happier frame of mind and on better terms with yourself, none of them will let you leave him empty-handed: yet their society may be enjoyed by all men, and by night as well as by day.

XV

None of these men will force you to die, but all of them will teach you how to die: none of these will waste your time, but will add his own to it. The talk of these men is not dangerous, their friendship will not lead you to the scaffold, their society will not ruin you in expenses: you may take from them whatsoever you will; they will not prevent your taking the deepest draughts of their wisdom that you please. What blessedness, what a fair old age awaits the man who takes these for his patrons! he will have friends with whom he may discuss all matters, great and small, whose advice he may ask daily about himself, from whom he will hear truth without insult, praise without flattery, and according to whose likeness he may model his own character. We are wont to say that we are not able to choose who our parents should be, but that they were assigned to us by chance; yet we may be born just as we please: there are several families of the noblest intellects: choose which you would like to belong to: by your adoption you will not receive their name only, but also their property, which is not intended to be guarded in a mean and miserly spirit: the more persons you divide it among the larger it becomes. These will open to you the path which leads to eternity, and will raise you to a height from whence none shall cast you down. By this means alone can you prolong your mortal life, nay, even turn it into an immortal one. High office, monuments, all that ambition records in decrees or piles up in stone, soon passes away: lapse of time casts down and ruins everything; but those things on which Philosophy has set its seal are beyond the reach of injury: no age will discard them or lessen their force, each succeeding century will add somewhat to the respect in which they are held: for we look upon what is near us with jealous eyes, but we admire what is further off with less prejudice. The wise man's life, therefore, includes much: he is not hedged in by the same limits which confine others: he alone is exempt from the laws by which mankind is governed: all ages serve him like a god. If any time be past, he recalls it by his memory; if it be present, he uses it; if it be future, he anticipates it: his life is a long one because he concentrates all times into it.

XVI

Those men lead the shortest and unhappiest lives who forget the past, neglect the present, and dread the future: when they reach the end of it the poor wretches learn too late that they were busied all the while that they were doing nothing. You need not think, because sometimes they call for death, that their lives are long: their folly torments them with vague passions which lead them into the very things of which they are afraid: they often, therefore, wish for death because they live in fear. Neither is it, as you might think, a proof of the length of their lives that they often find the days long, that they often complain how slowly the hours pass until the appointed time arrives for dinner: for whenever they are left without their usual business, they fret helplessly in their idleness, and know not how to arrange or to spin it out. They betake themselves, therefore, to some business, and all the intervening time is irksome to them; they would wish, by Hercules, to skip over it, just as they wish to skip over the intervening days before a gladiatorial contest or some other time appointed for a public spectacle or private indulgence: all postponement of what they wish for is grievous to them. Yet the very time which they enjoy is brief and soon past, and is made much briefer by their own fault: for they run from one pleasure to another, and are not able to devote themselves consistently to one passion: their days are not long, but odious to them: on the other hand, how short they find the nights which they spend with courtesans or over wine? Hence arises that folly of the poets who encourage the errors of mankind by their myths, and declare that Jupiter to gratify his voluptuous desires doubled the length of the night. Is it not adding fuel to our vices to name the gods as their authors, and to offer our distempers free scope by giving them deity for an example? How can the nights for which men pay so dear fail to appear of the shortest? they lose the day in looking forward to the night, and lose the night through fear of the dawn.

XVII

Such men's very pleasures are restless and disturbed by various alarms, and at the most joyous moment of all there rises the anxious thought: "How long will this last?" This frame of mind has led kings to weep over their power, and they have not been so much delighted at the grandeur of their position, as they have been terrified by the end to which it must some day come. That most arrogant Persian king,[1] when his army stretched over vast plains and could not be counted but only measured, burst into tears at the thought that in less than a hundred years none of all those warriors would be alive: yet their death was brought upon them by the very man who wept over it, who was about to destroy some of them by sea, some on land, some in battle, and some in flight, and who would in a very short space of time put an end to those about whose hundredth year he showed such solicitude. Why need we wonder at their very joys being mixed with fear? they do not rest upon any solid grounds, but are disturbed by the same emptiness from which they spring. What must we suppose to be the misery of such times as even they acknowledge to be wretched, when even the joys by which they elevate themselves and raise themselves above their fellows are of a mixed character. All the greatest blessings are enjoyed with fear, and no thing is so untrustworthy as extreme prosperity: we require fresh strokes of good fortune to enable us to keep that which we are enjoying, and even those of our prayers which are answered require fresh prayers. Everything for which we are dependent on chance is uncertain: the higher it rises, the more opportunities it has of falling. Moreover, no one takes any pleasure in what is about to fall into ruin: very wretched, therefore, as well as very short must be the lives of those who work very hard to gain what they must work even harder to keep: they obtain what they wish with infinite labour, and they hold what they have obtained with fear and trembling. Meanwhile they take no account of time, of which they will never have a fresh and larger supply: they substitute new occupations for old ones, one hope leads to another, one ambition to another: they do not seek for an end to their wretchedness, but they change its subject. Do our own preferments trouble us? nay, those of other men occupy more of our time. Have we ceased from our labours in canvassing? then we begin others in voting. Have we got rid of the trouble of accusation? then we begin that of judging. Has a man ceased to be a judge? then he becomes an examiner. Has he grown old in the salaried management of other people's property? then he becomes occupied with his own. Marius is discharged from military service; he becomes consul many times: Quintius is eager to reach the end of his dictatorship; he will be called a second time from the plough: Scipio marched against the Carthaginians before he was of years sufficient for so great an undertaking; after he has conquered Hannibal, conquered Antiochus, been the glory of his own consulship and the surety for that of his brother, he might, had he wished it, have been set on the same pedestal with Jupiter; but civil factions will vex the saviour of the State, and he who when a young man disdained to receive divine honours, will take pride as an old man in obstinately remaining in exile. We shall never lack causes of anxiety, either pleasurable or painful: our life will be pushed along from one business to another: leisure will always be wished for, and never enjoyed.

XVIII

Wherefore, my dearest Paulinus, tear yourself away from the common herd, and since you have seen more rough weather than one would think from your age, betake yourself at length to a more peaceful haven: reflect what waves you have sailed through, what storms you have endured in private life, and brought upon yourself in public. Your courage has been sufficiently displayed by many toilsome and wearisome proofs; try how it will deal with leisure: the greater, certainly the better part of your life, has been given to your country; take now some part of your time for yourself as well. I do not urge you to practise a dull or lazy sloth, or to drown all your fiery spirit in the pleasures which are dear to the herd: that is not rest: you can find greater works than all those which you have hitherto so manfully carried out, upon which you may employ yourself in retirement and security. You manage the revenues of the entire world, as unselfishly as though they belonged to another, as laboriously as if they were your own, as scrupulously as though they belonged to the public: you win love in an office in which it is hard to avoid incurring hatred; yet, believe me, it is better to understand your own mind than to understand the corn-market. Take away that keen intellect of yours, so well capable of grappling with the greatest subjects, from a post which may be dignified, but which is hardly fitted to render life happy, and reflect that you did not study from childhood all the branches of a liberal education merely in order that many thousand tons of corn might safely be entrusted to your charge: you have given us promise of something greater and nobler than this. There will never be any want of strict economists or of laborious workers: slow-going beasts of burden are better suited for carrying loads than well-bred horses, whose generous swiftness no one would encumber with a heavy pack. Think, moreover, how full of risk is the great task which you have undertaken: you have to deal with the human stomach: a hungry people will not endure reason, will not be appeased by justice, and will not hearken to any prayers. Only just a few days ago, when G. Caesar perished, grieving for nothing so much (if those in the other world can feel grief) as that the Roman people did not die with him, there was said to be only enough corn for seven or eight days' consumption: while he was making bridges with ships[1] and playing with the resources of the empire, want of provisions, the worst evil that can befall even a besieged city, was at hand: his imitation of a crazy outlandish and misproud king very nearly ended in ruin, famine, and the general revolution which follows famine. What must then have been the feelings of those who had the charge of supplying the city with corn, who were in danger of stoning, of fire and sword, of Gaius himself? With consummate art they concealed the vast internal evil by which the State was menaced, and were quite right in so doing; for some diseases must be cured without the patient's knowledge: many have died through discovering what was the matter with them.

XIX

Betake yourself to these quieter, safer, larger fields of action; do you think that there can be any comparison between seeing that corn is deposited in the public granary without being stolen by the fraud or spoilt by the carelessness of the importer, that it does not suffer from damp or overheating, and that it measures and weighs as much as it ought, and beginning the study of sacred and divine knowledge, which will teach you of what elements the gods are formed, what are their pleasures, their position, their form? to what changes your soul has to look forward? where Nature will place us when we are dismissed from our bodies? what that principle is which holds all the heaviest particles of our universe in the middle, suspends the lighter ones above, puts fire highest of all, and causes the stars to rise in their courses, with many other matters, full of marvels? Will you not[1] cease to grovel on Earth and turn your mind's eye on these themes? nay, while your blood still flows swiftly, before your knees grow feeble, you ought to take the better path. In this course of life there await you many good things, such as love and practice of the virtues, forgetfulness of passions, knowledge of how to live and die, deep repose. The position of all busy men is unhappy, but most unhappy of all is that of those who do not even labour at their own affairs, but have to regulate their rest by another man's sleep, their walk by another man's pace, and whose very love and hate, the freest things in the world, are at another's bidding. If such men wish to know how short their lives are, let them think how small a fraction of them is their own.

XX

When, therefore, you see a man often wear the purple robes of office, and hear his name often repeated in the forum, do not envy him: he gains these things by losing so much of his life. Men throw away all their years in order to have one year named after them as consul: some lose their lives during the early part of the struggle, and never reach the height to which they aspired: some after having submitted to a thousand indignities in order to reach the crowning dignity, have the miserable reflection that the only result of their labours will be the inscription on their tombstone. Some, while telling off extreme old age, like youth, for new aspirations, have found it fail from sheer weakness amid great and presumptuous enterprises. It is a shameful ending, when a man's breath deserts him in a court of justice, while, although well stricken in years, he is still striving to gain the sympathies of an ignorant audience for some obscure litigant: it is base to perish in the midst of one's business, wearied with living sooner than with working; shameful, too, to die in the act of receiving payments, amid the laughter of one's long-expectant heir. I cannot pass over an instance which occurs to me: Turannius was an old man of the most painstaking exactitude, who after entering upon his ninetieth year, when he had by Gr. Caesar's own act been relieved of his duties as collector of the revenue, ordered himself to be laid out on his bed and mourned for as though he were dead. The whole house mourned for the leisure of its old master, and did not lay aside its mourning until his work was restored to him. Can men find such pleasure in dying in harness? Yet many are of the same mind: they retain their wish for labour longer than their capacity for it, and fight against their bodily weakness; they think old age an evil for no other reason than because it lays them on the shelf. The law does not enroll a soldier after his fiftieth year, or require a senator's attendance after his sixtieth: but men have more difficulty in obtaining their own consent than that of the law to a life of leisure. Meanwhile, while they are plundering and being plundered, while one is disturbing another's repose, and all are being made wretched alike, life remains without profit, without pleasure, without any intellectual progress: no one keeps death well before his eyes, no one refrains from far-reaching hopes. Some even arrange things which lie beyond their own lives, such as huge sepulchral buildings, the dedication of public works, and exhibitions to be given at their funeral-pyre, and ostentatious processions: but, by Hercules, the funerals of such men ought to be conducted by the light of torches and wax tapers,[1] as though they had lived but a few days.

NOTES

DEDICATION

1. "On croit que ce Paulin étoit frère de Pauline, épouse de Sénéque."
   —La Grange

II

1. "L'un se consume en projets d'ambition, dont le succès dépend du suffrage de l'autrui." —La Grange
2. "Combien d'orateurs qui s'épuisent de sang et de forces pour faire montrer de leur génie!" —La Grange
3. "Pour vous, jamais vous ne daignâtes vous regarder seulement, ou vous entendre. Ne faites pas non plus valoir votre condescendance a écouter les autres. Lorsque vous vous y prétez, ce n'est pas que vous aimiez a vous communiquer aux autres; c'est que vous craignez de vous trouver avec vous-même." —La Grange.

"It is a folly therefore beyond Sence, When great men will not give us Audience To count them proud; how dare we call it pride When we the same have to ourselves deny'd.

Yet they how great, how proud so e're, have bin Sometimes so courteous as to call thee in, And hear thee speak; but thou could'st nere afford Thyself the leisure of a look or word.

Thou should'st not then herein another blame, Because when thou thyself do'st do the same, Thou would'st not be with others, but we see Plainly thou can'st not with thine own self be."

L. Annaeus Seneca, the Philosopher, his book of the Shortness of Life, translated into an English poem. Imprinted at London, by William Goldbird, for the Author.

IV

1. "Dans une lettre qu'il envoya au Sénat apres avoir promis que son repos n'aura rièn indigne de la gloire de ses premières années, il ajoute: Mais l'execution y mettra un prix, que ne peuvent y mettre les promesses. J'obeis cependant à la vive passion que j'ai, de me voir a ce temps si désiré; et puisque l'heureuse situation d'affaires m'en tient encore éloigné, j'ai voulu du moins me satisfaire en partie, par la douceur que je trouve à vous en parler." —La Grange
"Such words I find. But these things rather ought Be done, then said; yet so far hath the thought Of that wish'd time prevail'd, that though the glad Fruition of the thing be not yet had, Yet I," etc.

VII

1. The rods carried by the lictors as symbols of office. See Smith's Dictionary of Antiquities, s.v.

XIII

1. See Smith's Dictionary of Antiquities.

XVII

1. Xerxes.

XVIII

1. "Sénéque parle ici du pont que Caligula fit construire sur le golphe de Baies, l'an de Rome 791, 40 de J. C. ... Il rassembla et fit entrer dans la construction de son pont tous les vaisseaux qui se trouv-

erent dans les ports d'Italie et des contrées voisines. Il n'excepta pas même ceux qui etoient destinés a y apporter des grains étrangers," etc. —La Grange

XIX

1. For vis tu see Juvenal V, vis tu consuetis, etc. Mayor's note.

XX

1. As those of children were.